HBJ TREASURY OF LITERATURE

AT MY WINDOW

SENIOR AUTHORS
ROGER C. FARR
DOROTHY S. STRICKLAND

AUTHORS
RICHARD F. ABRAHAMSON
ELLEN BOOTH CHURCH
BARBARA BOWEN COULTER
MARGARET A. GALLEGO
JUDITH L. IRVIN
KAREN KUTIPER
JUNKO YOKOTA LEWIS
DONNA M. OGLE
TIMOTHY SHANAHAN
PATRICIA SMITH

SENIOR CONSULTANTS
BERNICE E. CULLINAN
W. DORSEY HAMMOND
ASA G. HILLIARD III

CONSULTANTS
ALONZO A. CRIM
ROLANDO R. HINOJOSA-SMITH
LEE BENNETT HOPKINS
ROBERT J. STERNBERG

HARCOURT BRACE & COMPANY
Orlando   Atlanta   Austin   Boston   San Francisco   Chicago   Dallas   New York
Toronto   London

Printed in the United States of America

ISBN 0-15-301357-5

3 4 5 6 7 8 9 10   048   96   95   94   93

Acknowledgments
For permission to reprint copyrighted material, grateful acknowledgment is made to the following sources:
Dutton Children's Books, a division of Penguin Books USA Inc.: Illustrations by Monica Wellington from *Who Is Tapping At My Window?* by A. G. Deming. Illustrations copyright © 1988 by Monica Wellington.
Ell-Bern Publishing Company (ASCAP): "The World Is Big, The World Is Small," lyrics and music by Ella Jenkins. Text copyright © 1966, assigned 1968 to Ella Jenkins.
HarperCollins Publishers: Who Took the Farmer's Hat? by Joan Nodset, illustrated by Fritz Siebel. Text copyright © 1963 by Joan M. Lexau; illustrations copyright © 1963 by Fritz Siebel.
Holt, Rinehart and Winston, Inc.: From *Round Is a Pancake* by Joan Sullivan. Text copyright © 1963 by Holt, Rinehart and Winston, Inc., renewed 1991 by Joan Sullivan.
Wayne A. Krows, on behalf of Jane W. Krows: "My House" by Jane W. Krows.
Little, Brown and Company: "Notice" from *One at a Time* by David McCord. Text copyright 1952 by David McCord.
Viking Penguin, a division of Penguin Books USA Inc.: From *A House Is a House for Me* by Mary Ann Hoberman. Text copyright © 1978 by Mary Ann Hoberman.
Walker Books Limited: Better Move On, Frog! by Ron Maris. © 1989 by Ron Maris.

Handwriting models in this program have been used with permission of the publisher, Zaner-Bloser, Inc., Columbus, OH.

Photograph Credits
6, HBJ/Maria Paraskevas; 24–25, HBJ Photo; 56, HBJ/Rich Franco; 70–71, HBJ/Maria Paraskevas; 84, HBJ/Rich Franco.

Illustration Credits

Table of Contents Art
Nathan Jarvis, lower left, 4, center, 4, 5; Roseanne Litzinger, upper left, 4; Gerald McDermott, far right, 5

Unit Opening Patterns
Tracy Sabin

Theme Opening Art
Roseanne Litzinger, 6, 7

Selection Art
Daryl Cagle, 8–9; Walter Stuart, 10–17; Roseanne Litzinger, 18–21; Nancy Woodman, 22–23; Ron Maris, 24–54; Carolyn Croll, 55; Monica Wellington, 56–67; Shirley Beckes, 68–69; Marcia Pyner, 72–73; Seymour Chwast, 74–79; Kathy Jeffers, 80–81; Linda Fennimore, 82–83; Fritz Siebel, 84–109; Bernard Most, 110–113; Kate Brennan Hall, 114–120.

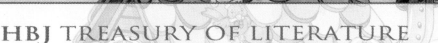

Dear Reader,

Open a window and let the wind
come in. Open a book and let the fun
begin. You'll find stories, poems, and
songs. You'll meet lots of children.
Get to know them and they can be
your friends. You might find that
they care about the same things
you do.

Stories, poems, and songs speak to
all of us all the time. So, let's get
started. Let's turn the page and meet
our new friends.

Sincerely,
The Authors

C O N T E N T S

ROUND AND ROUND / 70

6

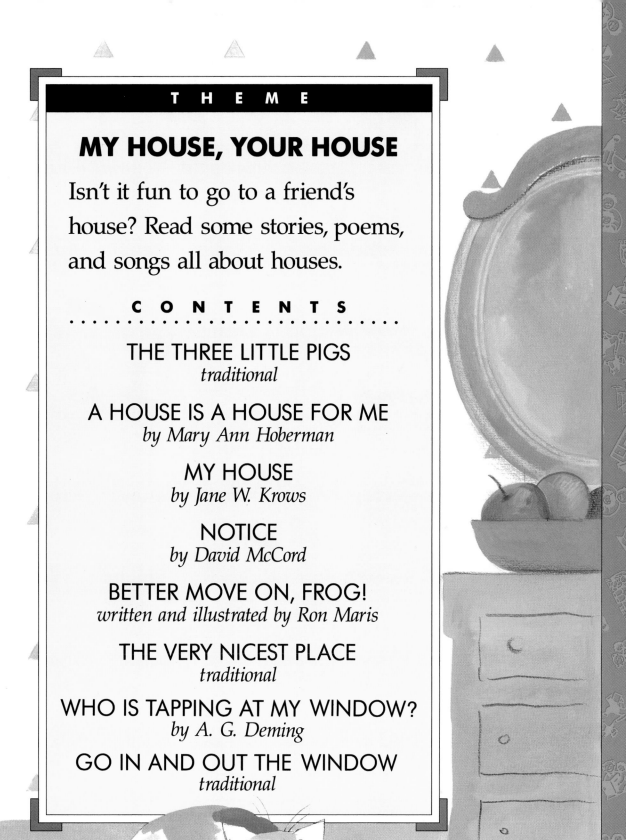

MY HOUSE, YOUR HOUSE

Isn't it fun to go to a friend's house? Read some stories, poems, and songs all about houses.

A HOUSE IS A HOUSE FOR ME

from a poem by
Mary Ann Hoberman
illustrated by Walter Stuart

A hill is a house
for an ant, an ant.

A hive is a house for a bee.

A hole is a house
for a mole or a mouse

And a house is a house for me!

A web is a house for a spider.

A bird builds its nest in a tree.

There is nothing so snug
as a bug in a rug

And a house is a house for me!

MY HOUSE

by Jane W. Krows

illustrated by Roseanne Litzinger

I have in my house
A door — a floor
A rug — a mug
A stool — a tool

A book — a nook
A stair — a chair
And I'll get
I bet — a pet.

CIRCUS

SHOW TONIGHT

NOTICE

I have a dog,
I have a cat.
I've got a frog
Inside my hat.

by David McCord
illustrated by
Nancy Woodman

AWARD-WINNING
POET

Better move on, Frog!

Ron Maris

24

Better move on, Frog!

by Ron Maris

SHARED READING

Holes! Lots of holes!
Which one shall I have?

Better move on, Frog.
This hole is full of badgers.

33

Better move on, Frog.
This hole is full of rabbits.

Better move on, Frog.
This hole is full of owls.

Better move on, Frog.
This hole is full of mice.

Better move on, Frog.
This hole is full of bees.

47

But look!

Better move in, Frog.
And wait for the hole to fill up . . .

. . . like all the other holes.

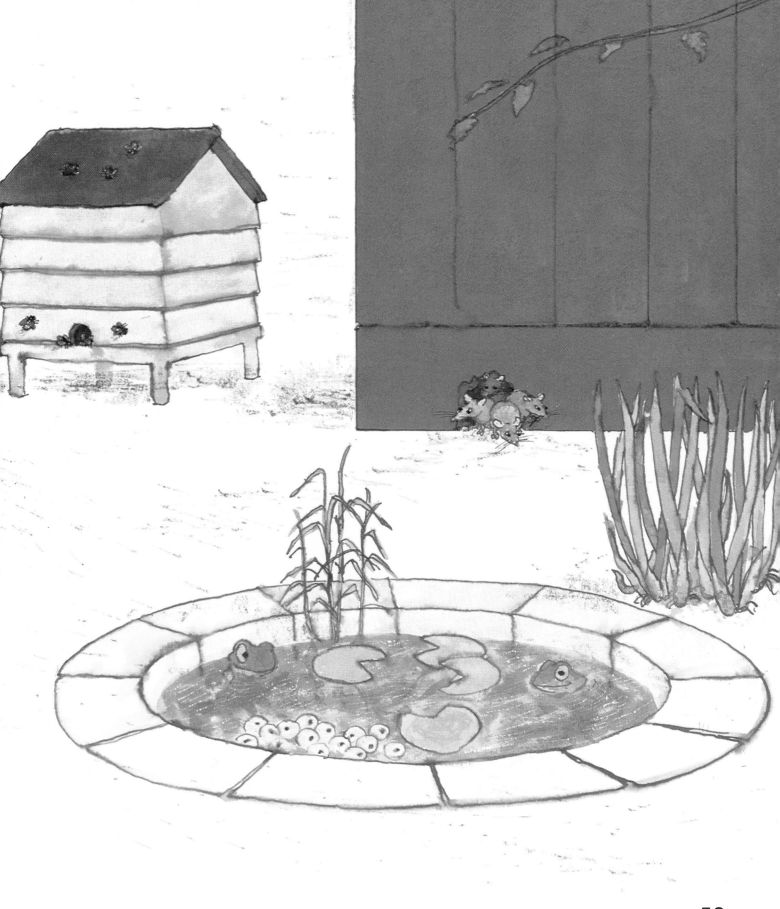

THE VERY NICEST PLACE

Author Unknown
illustrated by Carolyn Croll

The fish lives in the brook,
The bird lives in the tree,
But home's the very nicest place
For a little child like me.

55

Who is tapping at my window?

"It's not I," said the cat.

"It's not I," said the rat.

"It's not I," said the wren.

"It's not I," said the hen.

"It's not I," said the fox.

"It's not I," said the ox.

"It's not I,"
said the
loon.

"It's not I,"
said the
raccoon.

"It's not I,"
said the
cony.

"It's not I,"
said the
pony.

"It's not I,"
said the
dog.

"It's not I,"
said the
frog.

"It's not I," said the bear.

"It's not I," said the hare.

Who is tapping at my window?

"It is I," said the rain,

"tapping at your windowpane."

GO IN AND OUT THE WINDOW

A TRADITIONAL SONG

ILLUSTRATED BY SHIRLEY BECKES

Go in and out the
window,
Go in and out the
window,
Go in and out the
window,
As we have done
before.

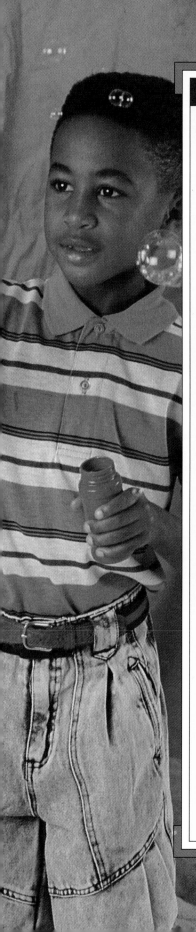

ROUND AND ROUND

How many things in the world are round? Are there too many to count? Let's read and find out.

C O N T E N T S

THE PANCAKE

An old tale

illustrated by Marcia Pyner

Stop, pancake!

73

ROUND IS A PANCAKE

illustrated by Seymour Chwast

Round is a pancake,
Round is a plum,
Round is a doughnut
And the top of a drum.

74

Round is a lollipop,

Round is a ring,

Round is a button

And the crown of a king.

Round is a bird's nest,
Round is a wheel,
Round is a daisy
And a fisherman's reel.

Round is a hamburger,
Round is a cake,
Round is a cherry
And the cookies we bake.

Round is a puppy
Curled up on a rug,
Round are the spots
On a wee ladybug.

Look all around you,
On the ground, in the air.
You will find round things
Everywhere.

MIX A PANCAKE

by Christina G. Rossetti
illustrated by Kathy Jeffers

Mix a pancake,
Stir a pancake,
Pop it in the pan;

Fry the pancake,
Toss the pancake,
Catch it if you can.

Mister

Oh Mister Sun, Sun, Mister Golden Sun,
Please shine down on me.
Oh Mister Sun, Sun, Mister Golden Sun,
Hiding behind a tree.

Sun

A traditional song
illustrated by Linda Fennimore

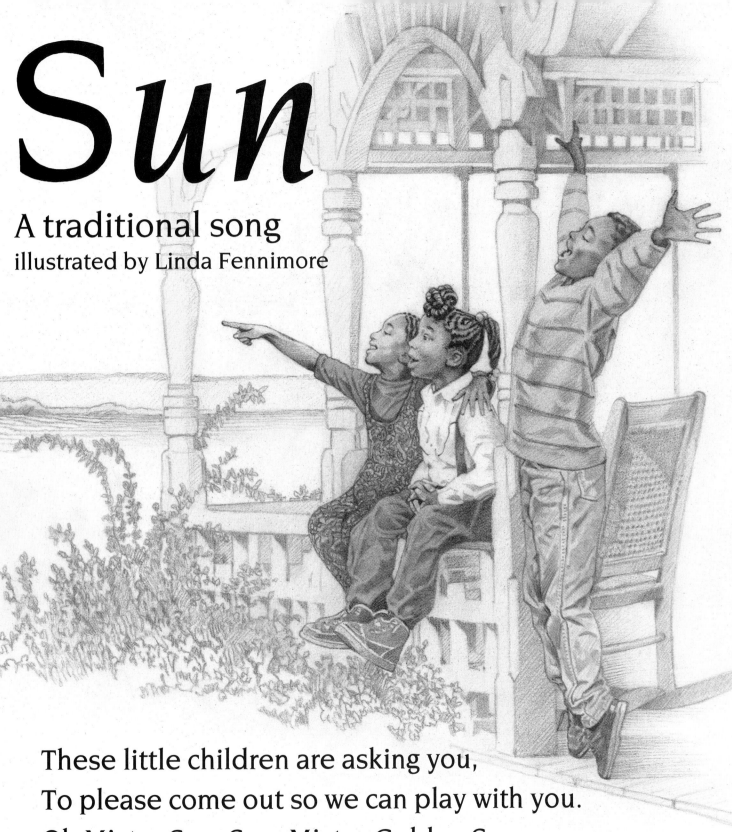

These little children are asking you,
To please come out so we can play with you.
Oh Mister Sun, Sun, Mister Golden Sun,
Please shine down on me.

Who Took The Farmer's Hat?

story by Joan L. Nodset • pictures by Fritz Siebel

The farmer had a hat, an old brown hat.

Oh, how he liked that old brown hat!

But the wind took it, and away it went.

The farmer ran fast, but the wind
went faster.

So the farmer had to look for it.

He looked and he looked

and he looked. No old brown hat.

He saw Squirrel. "Squirrel, did you
see my old brown hat?" said the
farmer.

"No," said Squirrel. "I saw a fat
round brown bird in the sky.
A bird with no wings."

The farmer saw Mouse. "Mouse,
did you see my old brown hat?"
said the farmer.

"No," said Mouse. "I saw a big
round brown mousehole in the
grass. I ran to it, but away it went."

The farmer saw Fly. "Fly, did you see my old brown hat?" said the farmer.

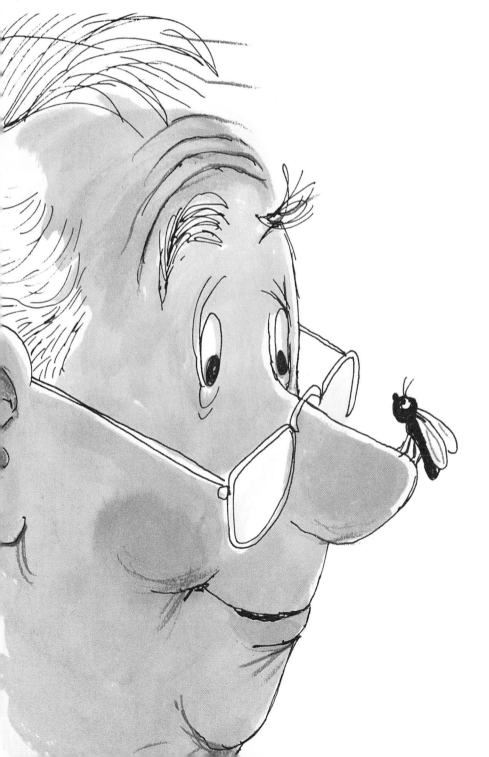

"No," said Fly. "I saw a flat round brown hill. The hill was in a tree. And then that hill took off, and away it went."

The farmer saw Goat. "Goat, did you see my old brown hat?" said the farmer.

"No," said Goat.

"I saw a funny round brown flowerpot.

I was going to eat it,

but the wind took that flowerpot away."

98

The farmer saw Duck. "Duck, did
you see my old brown hat?" said
the farmer.

"No," said Duck.
"I saw a silly round brown boat,
but Bird took that."

The farmer saw Bird.
"Bird, did you take
my old brown hat?"
said the farmer.

"No," said Bird.

"I saw this nice round brown nest,
but no hat."

The farmer looked
at the nest in the tree.
A nice old round
brown nest.

Bird was in it.

And an egg was in it.

"Oh, my!" said the farmer.

"Like it?" said Bird.

"I like it," said the farmer.

"Oh, yes, I like that nice round brown nest.

It looks a *little* like my old brown hat.

But I see it is a nice round brown nest."

The farmer has a new brown hat.

Oh, how he likes that new brown hat!

And how Bird likes that old brown nest!

What Will We Do

What will we do when we all go out,
All go out, all go out,
What will we do when we all go out,
When we all go out to play?

When We All Go Out?

illustrated by Bernard Most

We will walk in a zigzag line,
Walk in a zigzag line,
We will walk in a zigzag line
When we all go out to play.

What will we do when we all go out,
All go out, all go out,
What will we do when we all go out,
When we all go out to play?

We will jump like a kangaroo,
Jump like a kangaroo,
We will jump like a kangaroo
When we all go out to play.

THE WORLD IS
BIG
THE WORLD IS
small

By Ella Jenkins

illustrated by Kate Brennan Hall

Oh, the world is big,
And the world is small,
So there's lots of room
For the short and tall.

Oh, the world is far
And the world is wide,
But there are many different ways
To see the other side.

You can travel on a boat.
You can travel on a van.

You can travel on a jet.
You can travel on a train.

You can travel in a song.
You can travel in a book.